The Burnout Pattern

Why Therapists Exhaust Themselves—and How to Fix It

Hans Watson, DO

University Elite Press

Paperback ISBN: 978-1-972981-00-9
Hardcover ISBN: 978-1-972981-01-6
eBook ISBN: 978-1-972981-02-3

This book is intended for educational purposes only and is not a substitute for professional medical or mental health advice, diagnosis, or treatment.

First Edition

TABLE OF CONTENTS

Introduction

Quick Reference

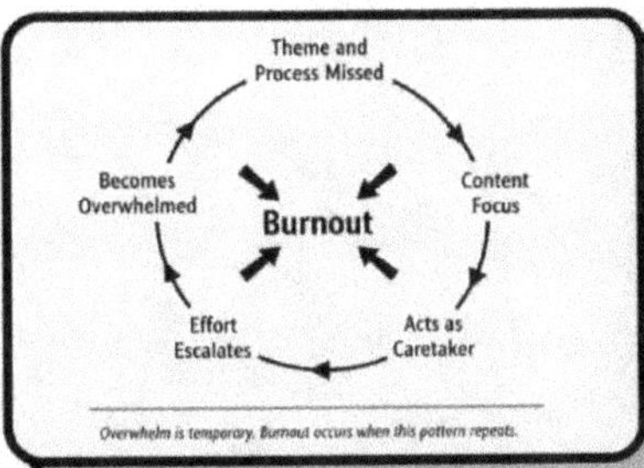

Mentor, *not* caretaker

Hurt (pain)
≠
harm (damage)

Theme and process first, content second

If I am working harder than the patient, the system is wrong

Am I reducing pain or building capacity?

Burnout is not caused by volume.

Burnout is caused by structural failure.

INTRODUCTION

The Burnout Pattern

"I can't do this anymore."

The comment sat at the top of a therapist forum thread and quickly began gaining traction, with the therapist who wrote it describing feeling overwhelmed, exhausted, and unable to continue under the demands of their current schedule. They explained that they were being asked to see more than twenty-five patients per week in order to maintain their benefits, and that the emotional toll of the work had become too much to sustain, leading them to conclude that expecting therapists to see more than twenty patients a week was unreasonable, even exploitative, given the intensity of the work.

Within minutes, the responses began to appear, with some agreeing and describing similar experiences of exhaustion while arguing that therapy was fundamentally different from other professions because sitting with people's pain, trauma, and distress all day created a level of emotional strain that could not be compared to other forms of work. Others disagreed just as strongly, pointing out that most practices could not sustain paying full-time salaries and benefits for twenty hours of work per week, and that the profession, like any other, required a balance between effort and output, with some suggesting that the issue was not simply the number of patients but how the work itself was being done.

The conversation quickly escalated, shifting from a discussion about burnout into an argument about fairness, expectations, and the nature of therapeutic work itself, with one side seeing the system as inherently exploitative and the other seeing the problem as a misunderstanding of what the work actually required. As the thread continued, the tone became increasingly divided, with each side questioning the other's assumptions, and like many of these conversations, it ended without resolution, leaving behind confusion rather than clarity and reinforcing competing explanations that all felt partially true yet insufficient on their own.

What you just read is not unusual, because conversations like this happen every day and reflect a widespread uncertainty about what burnout is, why it happens, and what actually needs to change in order to prevent it. At first glance, both sides of the argument appear to make valid points, since therapy is emotionally demanding work that requires sustained attention, deep engagement, and repeated exposure to difficult experiences, making it reasonable to assume that there must be a limit to how much of this a person can manage over time. The problem with this explanation, however, is that it does not account for a contradiction that becomes increasingly difficult to ignore.

Some therapists feel overwhelmed and burned out at relatively low caseloads, while others maintain clarity, energy, and effectiveness at significantly higher volumes, and if the primary issue were simply the number of patients being seen, this difference should not exist. While individual factors, including unresolved personal issues that may increase emotional reactivity in clinical work, can contribute to strain, they do not fully account for the consistent pattern observed across therapists. The fact that this difference persists suggests that something more fundamental is influencing how therapists experience their work, and understanding that difference becomes essential to understanding burnout itself.

In fact, this pattern is so common that on that same day I was working with a therapist who came to me with a similar concern, explaining that she felt increasingly overwhelmed in her work and was beginning to question whether the profession itself was sustainable. She had recently transitioned from training into a full-time clinical role, and while we initially discussed the normal adjustment period that comes with increased volume and responsibility, it became clear over time that what she was experiencing was not simply acclimation. Despite gaining experience, the work continued to feel heavier, and the effort required to maintain it continued to increase, which raised a different question: if burnout were simply a function of workload, why was it not resolving with experience?

This book will allow you to follow her progression, not as a case study to be analyzed in isolation, but as a practical illustration of how burnout develops and how it can be corrected when the structure of the work changes. The patterns that emerged in her work are the same patterns reflected in the conversation above, and they provide a clear example of how therapists can move from confusion and exhaustion to clarity and sustainability.

Introduction

Before going further, it is important to acknowledge something that is often overlooked, which is that there is a natural period of adjustment that occurs when therapists move from training into full-time clinical work. During this transition, it is common to experience fatigue, cognitive strain, and early signs that resemble burnout, and in many cases, this reflects adaptation rather than failure, as therapists gradually become more efficient and organized with experience. At the same time, not all burnout resolves with experience, and one of the central questions this book will address is why some therapists improve over time while others continue to experience increasing strain despite gaining more experience.

That distinction is grounded in lived experience as well as observation, because early in my own career I encountered the same patterns described here, where the work felt heavier than it should have and increasing effort did not make it more sustainable. Through training and supervising other therapists, it became clear that this experience was not universal, as some therapists developed clarity and efficiency while others became increasingly overwhelmed despite working just as hard, revealing that the difference was not effort, intelligence, or dedication, but structure.

What follows may challenge some assumptions, because the approach taken here is not based on what feels fair or unfair, or on what seems right or wrong in the moment, but on what consistently produces results over time. While there are other factors that can contribute to burnout, including medical, personal, and situational variables, the focus of this book is on the most consistent and controllable driver observed in clinical work: the structure of how therapy is practiced. There are many approaches in therapy that sound compassionate and feel appropriate but fail to produce meaningful and consistent change, and when something does not work, continuing to do it—no matter how well intentioned—will inevitably create problems, one of which is burnout.

Burnout is not primarily caused by how much you work, but by how you are working, and over time a consistent reality emerges when observing therapists in practice. Therapists are not burning out because they care too much, but because they are practicing in a way that does not work, which leads them to take on responsibility for outcomes they do not control, focus on solving individual situations rather than identifying patterns, and work harder than the patient in an attempt to create progress. At the same time, what appears on the surface as a series of unrelated problems is often being organized by a deeper structure that determines how those experiences are interpreted and responded to, and when that structure is not recognized, the therapist is left managing an ever-expanding set of situations without a clear way to resolve them.

As this continues, the cost becomes clear, because the effort required to sustain the work increases while the effectiveness of the work becomes inconsistent, and sessions begin to feel heavier as the same types of problems continue to appear in different forms. This progression is not random but follows a pattern, and the purpose of this book is to make that pattern visible so that once it is clearly understood, it can be recognized, interrupted, and ultimately prevented.

Preventing burnout does not require lowering standards, reducing meaningful work, or becoming emotionally detached from patients, because when therapy is structured correctly, therapists are able to be more present, more focused, and more effective while maintaining sustainability. This reflects a shift away from viewing burnout as a self-care issue and toward understanding it as a structural issue, where the way the work is organized determines whether it becomes sustainable or exhausting.

As you read, you may begin to recognize patterns in your own work, and some of those realizations may feel uncomfortable, but that discomfort often signals that something important is becoming clearer. Avoiding discomfort, whether in patients or in ourselves, is one of the primary ways that ineffective therapy and burnout are maintained, which makes the ability to tolerate and understand discomfort essential to both growth and sustainability.

The goal of this book is not to criticize but to clarify, and if you are willing to examine your work honestly, you will gain the ability to work at a high level while maintaining your energy over time. Once the burnout pattern becomes clear, the process of changing it becomes equally clear, allowing the work to become both effective and sustainable in a way that is not dependent on reducing effort but on structuring it correctly.

CHAPTER 1

Why Therapists Think They Burnout

Therapists do not arrive at burnout by accident. They usually arrive there by acting on a set of beliefs that feel logical, are widely shared, and are rarely challenged.

The conversation described in the introduction is not an isolated example. It reflects a belief system that has become increasingly common among therapists, where burnout is understood primarily as a function of workload. Many believe that the emotional intensity of the work creates a natural ceiling, and that exceeding that ceiling inevitably leads to exhaustion. Over time, this belief becomes accepted as truth, not because studies support that conclusion, but because it is repeated often enough that it begins to feel self-evident.

This belief is reinforced in multiple ways. It appears in training programs that correctly emphasize the emotional toll of the profession, in professional conversations where that truth is incorrectly portrayed as the driver of burnout becoming an expected outcome, and in peer discussions where therapists compare caseload limits as though those limits are fixed realities rather than variables shaped by how the therapy approach is applied. As this belief is repeated, it begins to shape not only how therapists think about burnout, but how they interpret their own experience of the work.

At first glance, the assumption that burnout is a product of excessive therapy sessions appears reasonable. Therapists sit with pain every day, listening to trauma, loss, conflict, and uncertainty, while being expected to remain present and engaged in situations that rarely have simple solutions. It is correct to conclude that if done inefficiently, there is a limit to how much of this a person can sustain. However, this explanation does not account for an insight that is becoming increasingly difficult to ignore, and that insight makes a significant difference in whether burnout develops.

Some therapists feel overwhelmed and depleted at relatively low caseloads, while others maintain clarity, energy, and effectiveness at significantly higher volumes, and if the emotional content within therapy sessions were the primary cause of burnout, this difference should not exist. The fact that it does suggests that something else is influencing whether therapists experience burnout, and understanding that difference becomes essential to understanding the problem itself.

The therapist I was supervising was working from the same assumption that burnout was simply a result of high caseloads. As her caseload increased, she began to feel the emotional strain that many clinicians describe, and like those in the forum discussion, her initial conclusion was that the volume itself must be the problem. In a supervision session, she brought in a case that felt particularly overwhelming and explained that the session had left her feeling burned out. When asked to describe what had happened, she outlined in detail the different issues the patient was facing, including the recent loss of a dog that had become an important source of comfort, the growing distance from a son who was becoming more independent and less responsive to calls and messages, a lack of meaningful friendships, and a sense that work felt empty and disconnected from any deeper purpose.

As the therapist I was supervising described these experiences, it became clear that she was tracking the details of each situation individually, trying to understand what had happened in each one and what might be done to improve it, while becoming increasingly overwhelmed by the number of details she was trying to manage. Each situation felt significant on its own, and the more attention that was given to those details, the more complex the patient's situation appeared to become. At a certain point, I shifted the focus away from what was happening in each situation to whether there was something that connected all of them, and when asked what tied these experiences together, she was unable to identify a single connecting thread that could account for the pattern as a whole. What she could see clearly was the content, but what was not yet visible was the underlying thread, which we will refer to as the theme. Additionally, she was unable to see how the patient was interpreting these experiences in a way that organized them into a single theme, which served as the patient's attempt to explain her current life situation.

At this point, I could see how she was assuming her feelings of burnout were driven by one of the most common assumptions therapists make, which is that emotional exposure is the primary driver of burnout. This assumption leads therapists to believe that the more pain they encounter in session, the more exhausted they will become, and it creates a subtle but important shift in how the work is approached when multiple emotionally charged situations are present in a patient's life. Instead of focusing on identifying the underlying theme and understanding how the patient is interpreting that theme, therapists often become pulled into managing the details of each situation, which leads to an increased focus on content and a shift toward reducing discomfort in the moment rather than helping the patient understand the patterns shaping their experience.

At first, the attempt to prioritize reduction of discomfort feels appropriate and aligned with the therapist's intention to help, but it is also the point where the system begins to break down. When therapy's primary focus becomes managing the patient's experience instead of understanding the underlying theme and the process through which that theme is interpreted, the therapist begins taking on responsibility that does not belong to them, and the work becomes heavier, not because the problems themselves are more severe, but because the therapist has moved into a role that requires doing something that cannot be sustained.

There is a principle in medicine that captures this distinction clearly. In *The House of God*, Samuel Shem writes that "the patient is the one with the disease," a statement that highlights the reality that the patient is the one who must ultimately live with, confront, and change the patterns that are creating the difficulty. The clinician's role is to guide, to teach, and to provide structure, but not to carry the condition for them, and when this distinction is lost, the therapist begins to feel responsible not just for guiding the process, but for the outcome itself.

This shift changes everything, because as the therapist begins to work harder on solving individual situations, think more about each detail of content, and invest more emotional energy in an attempt to produce results, the increased effort does not solve the problem and instead contributes to burnout. At the same time, the continued focus on content often prevents the therapist from recognizing the underlying theme and the process through which the patient is interpreting that theme, leaving the therapist without a clear organizing framework for understanding what is happening.

This creates an endless loop in which each session introduces new details, each situation feels different, and the therapist is forced to create a new intervention for each problem. Because the underlying theme and the process used to interpret that theme have not been identified, the therapist is presented with an amount of information that becomes increasingly difficult to organize effectively, and the effort required to sustain the work becomes excessive.

Over time, several things begin to happen simultaneously. The therapist's effort increases to unsustainable levels, and in an attempt to keep all the information organized, the therapist begins thinking excessively about patients outside of sessions, which often results in emotional fatigue and decreased effectiveness rather than improvement. The therapist I was supervising began to recognize this pattern, noticing that the harder she tried to remember each detail, the less clear the work became, and she began to see that the sense of burnout she was experiencing was directly related to the inability to organize what she was observing into a coherent framework.

It would take time before she fully internalized the reality that the combination of high effort and inconsistent progress is one of the most powerful drivers of burnout, not because the therapist does not care, but because the therapist is working in a way that cannot produce reliable outcomes. As this continues, many therapists follow the same logical but incorrect conclusion, assuming that the problem is the workload and attempting to solve it by reducing their caseload, taking more time off, or creating more space between sessions. While this may provide temporary relief, it does not address the underlying issue, because the therapy approach has not changed, and when the workload increases again, the same patterns generally re-emerge.

Burnout, in this sense, is not a reflection of weakness, but a reflection of a system that is not aligned with how change actually occurs. When therapists are taught to focus primarily on content, manage emotional experience, and take responsibility for outcomes, they are being set up to work in a way that is inherently inefficient and unsustainable, and the solution is not to reduce effort but to reorganize how that effort is applied.

When the therapy approach is correct, the therapist no longer attempts to solve every situation and does not absorb responsibility for outcomes, but instead identifies patterns, understands the underlying themes those patterns are built around, and helps the patient develop the capacity to respond differently. As this shift occurs, the work becomes lighter, not because it matters less or because the therapist is doing less, but because the therapist is working more efficiently within a framework that allows the work to make sense.

This leads to the central principle that frames everything that follows: burnout is not caused by caring too much, but by how therapy is practiced, which means that once the therapy approach changes, the experience of the work changes as well.

CHAPTER 1 — SUMMARY

- A common belief system assumes workload is the primary cause of burnout
- Emotional intensity alone does not explain why some therapists burn out and others do not
- Therapists often focus on content instead of recognizing the underlying theme and process
- When focus remains primarily on content, responsibility for outcomes gradually shifts from the patient to the therapist
- Increased inefficient effort results in burnout, not better outcomes
- Burnout reflects a failure in how therapy is practiced, not a failure of the therapist

CHAPTER 2

Why That Explanation Is Incomplete

If burnout were primarily caused by workload, the pattern would be predictable. As the number of patients increased, burnout would increase in a consistent and measurable way, and reducing the number of sessions would reliably resolve the problem. This assumption underlies many of the recommendations given to therapists who are struggling, and it explains why burnout is often framed as an issue of volume rather than of how therapy is practiced.

The difficulty is that this pattern does not hold up under closer examination. Some therapists experience significant burnout at relatively low caseloads, while others maintain clarity, effectiveness, and engagement at substantially higher volumes, and if workload alone were the primary cause of burnout, this difference should not exist. [1] The presence of this inconsistency suggests that something more fundamental is influencing how therapists experience their work.

The therapist I was supervising was encountering this contradiction directly. At the time she began to feel burned out, her caseload was not excessive by most professional standards, yet the strain she experienced was significant. Her initial response was logical, as she began to consider whether reducing her workload would solve the problem, but as we reviewed her sessions, it became clear that the difficulty she was encountering was not limited to how many patients she was seeing, but to how she was engaging with each patient.

In session, her effort was disproportionately high. She was attempting to track each detail, understand every situation, and generate an appropriate response for each new problem as it appeared, and because she had not yet developed the ability to consistently recognize the underlying theme and the way each patient was interpreting that theme, every situation required fresh analysis. This meant that even a moderate caseload could produce a level of cognitive and emotional demand that felt unsustainable.

This is where the workload explanation begins to break down. When therapists experience high effort combined with inconsistent outcomes, the work becomes exhausting regardless of the number of sessions. The issue is not simply how much work is being done, but whether the therapy approach being used allows that work to produce reliable results. When the approach is inefficient, increasing effort does not consistently improve outcomes, and the therapist is forced to compensate by investing more time, attention, and emotional energy into each case.

This creates a cycle that appears to confirm the original belief while quietly reinforcing the actual problem. The therapist becomes overwhelmed and reduces workload, which temporarily relieves pressure because fewer sessions reduce the immediate demand, and for a period of time, the work feels more manageable. This reinforces the belief that workload is the primary issue, even though the underlying therapy approach has not changed.

When the therapist returns to a higher caseload, the same patterns re-emerge. The cognitive load increases, the effort required to manage each case rises, and the sense of overwhelm returns, often more quickly than before. This pattern reveals something important: reducing workload may reduce symptoms, but it does not resolve the cause.

At this point, the explanation becomes incomplete. If decreasing workload temporarily reduces burnout but does not prevent it from returning, then workload cannot be the primary driver. What this suggests instead is that the system being used to approach the work is not producing consistent results, and when a system does not produce reliable outcomes, the only available response is to increase effort.

This is where burnout begins to accelerate. As effort increases without a corresponding increase in effectiveness, the therapist begins to invest more energy into thinking about patients between sessions, replaying interactions, and attempting to refine their approach in increasingly detailed ways. While this may produce short-term improvements, it does not correct the underlying inefficiency, because the therapy approach itself remains unchanged. Over time, this leads to increased cognitive load, decreased clarity, and diminished effectiveness, which has been consistently associated with poorer patient outcomes. [1]

The therapist I was supervising began to recognize this pattern in her own work. Even when she reduced her schedule temporarily, the mental burden associated with each session remained high, and as soon as her caseload increased again, the same sense of overwhelm returned. This made it clear that the issue was not simply how much she was working, but how the work was structured within each session.

When effort increases without improving outcomes, the system becomes unsustainable. The therapist continues to invest more energy in an attempt to maintain progress, but because the underlying approach has not been corrected, the gap between effort and effectiveness continues to widen. Eventually, that gap becomes too large to maintain, and what began as manageable strain develops into burnout.

Understanding this changes how burnout is interpreted. Burnout is not simply a function of how much work is being done, but a reflection of whether the work is being done in a way that produces consistent and reliable results. When the therapy approach is aligned with how change occurs, effort becomes more efficient, responsibility is appropriately distributed, and the work becomes sustainable. When the approach is misaligned, the therapist becomes the primary driver of progress, and the system begins to break down.

This is the point at which burnout becomes predictable. When the traditional explanation no longer fits the observed reality, a different explanation is required, and identifying that explanation becomes the next step.

CHAPTER 2 — SUMMARY

- Burnout occurs inconsistently across therapists with similar caseloads
- Reducing workload provides temporary relief but does not resolve the problem
- High effort combined with inconsistent outcomes drives burnout
- Inefficient therapy approaches force therapists to compensate through effort
- Burnout becomes predictable when effort increases without improving effectiveness

CHAPTER 3

The Hidden Variable

By this point, something should feel incomplete. The workload explanation has been tested and does not hold up consistently, and while reducing the number of sessions may temporarily reduce strain, it does not resolve the underlying problem. The therapist continues to experience the same patterns of overwhelm, effort continues to increase, and the work continues to feel heavier than it should, which suggests that something essential is still missing from the explanation.

That missing element is not immediately obvious, because it is not something that presents itself directly in the session. What is most visible in therapy is the content of a patient's life, including the events, conversations, and circumstances that the patient brings into the room, and it is natural for both the therapist and the patient to focus on those details. However, what is visible is not always what is most important, and when attention remains focused on the surface of what is happening, the deeper structure that organizes those experiences remains hidden, often requiring a more developed level of clinical skill to recognize.

The therapist I was supervising encountered this directly. After recognizing that the number of sessions alone did not explain her sense of burnout, she began to question why the work felt so difficult to manage, and in supervision we returned to the same case that had originally led her to feel overwhelmed. As we reviewed the session again, the details were still present, including the loss of the dog, the distance from the patient's son, the absence of meaningful friendships, and the lack of fulfillment in work, and each of those elements still carried emotional weight. What had changed was not the content itself, but the question being asked about it.

Instead of asking what needed to be solved in each situation, the focus shifted toward what connected those situations and how the patient was making sense of them. At that point, it became possible to identify something that had not been visible before, which was that all of the different experiences being described were connected by a single underlying theme centered on the patient's struggle to establish and maintain meaningful social connection. This theme was not always stated directly, but it was present in each situation and provided a unifying explanation for why the different problems felt so significant.

At the same time, it became clear that the patient was not simply experiencing this theme, but was interpreting it in a particular way. Rather than recognizing the lack of connection as something that could be understood and addressed, the patient was interpreting these experiences through a process that framed others as unkind or rejecting, which allowed the patient to see themselves as a victim of circumstances rather than as an active participant in shaping those circumstances. This interpretation organized the content into a coherent narrative, but it also reinforced the pattern that was creating the difficulty in the first place.

This distinction introduces the missing variable in understanding burnout, because what the therapist had been managing was not just the content of the patient's life, but a system made up of three interacting elements: the underlying theme that organizes the patient's experience, the way that theme is interpreted, and the content that is used to support that interpretation. When these elements are not recognized together, the therapist is left trying to manage an ever-expanding set of details without a clear way to organize or resolve them, and without the ability to identify these three elements, the therapist is unable to recognize patterns as they occur in real time or bring them into the room in a way that allows the patient to become aware of them.

Content, by itself, is infinite. There are always more details, more situations, and more variables that can be considered, and when therapy is focused at this level, each new problem requires additional attention and effort. Theme and process, however, are limited. They repeat across situations, they organize how those situations are understood, and they determine how the patient responds, which means that when they are identified correctly, they provide a way to understand many situations at once rather than addressing each one individually.

The therapist I was supervising began to see this difference as we continued reviewing her sessions. What initially appeared to be a series of unrelated problems began to feel familiar, because once the underlying theme and the way that theme was being interpreted became visible, each new situation could be understood within the same framework. Instead of requiring a new explanation for each problem, the work became focused on helping the patient recognize the pattern that was already present.

This shift did not eliminate effort, but it changed where that effort was directed. Instead of attempting to solve each individual situation, the therapist began selecting the most useful moments within the session to help the patient understand the theme that was organizing the experience and the way that theme was being interpreted. As this happened, the amount of information that the therapist needed to manage decreased, her sense of overwhelm began to lessen, the patient started progressing, and the work started to feel more structured and more sustainable.

This is why the workload explanation fails. It assumes that the difficulty of therapy is determined by the number of problems being addressed, when in reality the difficulty is determined by whether those problems are being organized in a way that allows them to be understood and resolved. When theme and process are not identified, the therapist is forced to manage content alone, which creates an unsustainable level of complexity. When theme and process are recognized, the same work becomes more efficient, more predictable, and more manageable.

At this point, the direction of the solution becomes clearer, because if burnout is not caused by how much work is being done, but by how that work is being approached, then the focus must shift from reducing workload to correcting the underlying framework through which therapy is practiced.

CHAPTER 3 — SUMMARY

- Each patient's experience is organized by an underlying theme
- That theme is interpreted through a consistent process
- Content reflects and reinforces that interpretation
- Without recognizing theme and process, patterns cannot be brought into the room
- Recognizing theme and process allows multiple problems to be understood within a single framework

CHAPTER 4

The Burnout Pattern

By this point, the underlying structure of the problem should be clear. Burnout is not simply the result of working too much, and it is not explained by emotional intensity alone. It develops when the therapy approach is not aligned with how patients organize and interpret their experiences, which creates a predictable pattern that unfolds over time.

This pattern begins when the underlying theme and the way that theme is being interpreted are not recognized. Without that organizing framework, attention naturally shifts to content, and each situation is treated as a separate problem that must be understood and resolved on its own. The therapist I was supervising experienced this directly, as each session required tracking new details, analyzing different circumstances, and attempting to generate solutions for problems that appeared unrelated. Without a unifying framework, the amount of information that needed to be managed increased rapidly, and the work began to feel more complex than it actually was.

As this continued, she attempted to create continuity across sessions by revisiting previous situations and evaluating whether the strategies she and the patient had developed were working. This instinct was correct in principle, but without a clearly identified theme, those connections were based on content rather than structure. As a result, the patient experienced these attempts as disconnected from the current problem, and instead of feeling understood, the patient became increasingly frustrated that attention was being directed toward past situations when new ones were emerging. What appeared to be a reasonable effort to create coherence instead highlighted the absence of a unifying framework, and the work began to feel disjointed for both the therapist and the patient.

This is one of the ways the pattern reveals itself. When theme and process are not identified, even appropriate clinical instincts can produce unintended consequences, because the therapist is attempting to create connections without a structure that makes those connections meaningful. Without it, continuity feels forced rather than natural, and both the therapist and the patient experience the work as fragmented.

The Burnout Pattern

As the therapist continues working at the level of content, responsibility inevitably shifts onto the therapist. Because each situation requires separate attention and response, the therapist becomes the primary organizer of the session, deciding what matters, what should be addressed, and what should be done next. This shift is subtle, but it marks a transition from guiding the process to managing the patient's experience, and once that transition occurs, the balance of effort within the session begins to change.

With responsibility shifting toward the therapist, effort begins to escalate until the therapist is working harder than the patient, which is one of the clearest indicators that the system has become inefficient. The therapist works harder to understand each detail, invests more time thinking about patients between sessions, and attempts to maintain clarity across an expanding set of variables. At the same time, the lack of a unifying framework prevents that effort from producing consistent results, which creates a growing gap between how much work is being done and how effective that work actually is.

As effort increases without improving outcomes, the therapist begins to experience overwhelm. This is often the first point at which burnout becomes noticeable, because the cognitive and emotional demand of the work has exceeded what can be sustained. However, at this stage, overwhelm is still an acute response to an inefficient system rather than a permanent condition, and because it is experienced subjectively, it is often attributed to workload or emotional exposure rather than to the underlying structure of the work itself.

The most common acute response to this experience is to increase effort even further or to attempt to reduce workload. Both responses are understandable, but neither addresses the underlying issue. Increasing effort amplifies the problem by placing more demand on an already inefficient system, while reducing workload may temporarily relieve pressure without correcting the structure that created it. As a result, the same pattern continues to repeat, and each time it does, the therapist returns to the same position more quickly.

This is the point at which burnout develops. When the pattern is repeated over time, what begins as intermittent overwhelm becomes a chronic state, and the therapist's ability to maintain clarity, energy, and effectiveness begins to decline. At this stage, burnout is no longer a temporary response but the predictable outcome of a system that cannot sustain itself.

This entire sequence can be understood as a single, predictable pattern that connects each stage. When the underlying theme and the process through which that theme is interpreted are not recognized, the therapist defaults to content. As content becomes the focus, responsibility shifts toward the therapist. As responsibility increases, effort escalates. As effort escalates without improving outcomes, overwhelm develops. When this pattern repeats, burnout becomes inevitable.

Understanding this pattern is critical, because it shifts the focus from managing symptoms to correcting the system that produces them. Burnout is not something that needs to be endured or managed indefinitely. It is something that can be predicted, recognized, and prevented by changing how therapy is practiced.

CHAPTER 4 — SUMMARY

- Each patient's experience is organized by an underlying theme
- That theme is interpreted through a consistent process
- Content reflects and reinforces the process used to interpret the theme
- Without recognizing theme and process, patterns cannot be brought into the room
- Recognizing theme and process allows multiple problems to be understood within a single framework

CHAPTER 5

Caretaker vs Mentor

By the time the burnout pattern becomes visible, the therapist is often already operating within a role that is different from the one they were originally trained to perform. This shift does not occur abruptly, but emerges gradually as the therapist attempts to manage increasing complexity without a unifying framework, and over time it changes both how the work is structured and how the therapist experiences that work.

Therapists typically enter the profession with the intention of helping patients develop the ability to navigate their lives more effectively, which places them in a role that is best understood as that of a mentor. In this role, the therapist focuses on identifying patterns, helping the patient understand the underlying theme that organizes those patterns, and guiding the patient toward developing the capacity to respond differently outside of the session. The therapist provides structure and clarity, but does not assume responsibility for producing outcomes.

When the therapy approach becomes misaligned, this role begins to change. As described in the previous chapter, when theme and process are not identified, attention shifts toward content, and each situation is treated as a separate problem that must be addressed. As the number of problems increases, the therapist begins to take on responsibility for organizing the session, maintaining continuity, and ensuring that progress is being made, which creates a subtle but important shift in how the therapist defines success.

The therapist I was supervising began to experience this shift as the complexity of her sessions increased. Without a clear understanding of the underlying theme and the process organizing the patient's experiences, she began to evaluate her effectiveness based on whether she was able to resolve one or more of the situations presented in each session. If a session ended without a clear resolution to at least one of those problems, she experienced that as a failure on her part, which led to a growing sense of pressure to produce measurable progress each time she met with a patient.

As this pattern continued, the therapist began to feel responsible not only for understanding what was happening, but for ensuring that something was fixed during each session. When progress did not occur in the way she expected, she experienced guilt and began to question whether she was doing enough, which led her to invest even more effort into trying to solve the problems being presented. What she did not yet recognize was that she was attempting to control something she could not directly control, because the patient's life was not limited to the session, and the situations she was trying to resolve were the result of patterns that would continue to generate new problems over time.

This is the point at which the therapist moves into the caretaker role. In this role, the therapist becomes the primary driver of the work, taking on responsibility for outcomes, attempting to stabilize the patient's emotional experience, and working to ensure that each situation is addressed in a way that reduces distress. While this approach is often motivated by a desire to help, it changes the structure of the work in a way that makes it increasingly difficult to sustain.

The caretaker role creates a system in which the therapist must continuously respond to the patient's needs in real time, adjusting to new situations, managing emotional reactions, and attempting to maintain progress across an expanding set of variables. Because the underlying theme and process are not being used to organize the work, each situation remains separate, and the therapist is required to generate a response for each one. Over time, this leads to an increase in cognitive load, emotional investment, and overall effort, which reinforces the burnout pattern described in the previous chapter.

In contrast, the mentor role operates within a different structure. Instead of managing the patient's experience, the therapist focuses on helping the patient understand the underlying theme and the way that theme is being interpreted, which allows the patient to recognize patterns and apply that understanding across multiple situations. In this role, the therapist is responsible for guiding the process, but not for producing the outcome, and the patient retains responsibility for applying what is learned outside of the session.

The difference between these roles becomes most visible in how responsibility is distributed. In the caretaker role, responsibility shifts toward the therapist, who becomes increasingly involved in managing the details of the patient's life and the outcomes of those situations. In the mentor role, responsibility is appropriately shared, with the therapist providing structure and insight while the patient remains responsible for change. This distinction is not theoretical, because it directly affects how much effort the therapist must expend and how sustainable that effort becomes over time.

The therapist I was supervising began to recognize this distinction as she continued to review her sessions. She noticed that the more she attempted to resolve individual situations, the more problems appeared, and the more effort was required to keep up with them. As she shifted her focus toward identifying patterns and helping the patient understand the underlying theme, the pressure to resolve each situation began to decrease, and the work started to feel more organized. Instead of measuring success by whether a specific problem was solved, she began to recognize that helping the patient see the pattern itself was the more meaningful form of progress.

This shift did not eliminate effort, but it changed how effort was applied. In the caretaker role, effort is used to manage complexity and produce outcomes, while in the mentor role, effort is used to create clarity and guide understanding. When clarity increases, complexity decreases, and the work becomes more efficient, more predictable, and more sustainable.

The burnout pattern described in the previous chapter is directly tied to this role shift. When the therapist is functioning as a caretaker, the pattern is reinforced, because responsibility continues to move toward the therapist, effort continues to increase, and overwhelm develops more quickly. When the therapist is functioning as a mentor, the pattern is interrupted, because the focus shifts to identifying the underlying structure, responsibility is redistributed, and the work becomes more manageable.

Understanding this distinction reframes burnout as a role problem rather than a workload problem. The question is no longer how many patients the therapist is seeing, but how the therapist is engaging with those patients and whether that engagement is aligned with a role that allows the work to function effectively. When therapists remain in the mentor role, they are able to sustain higher levels of engagement without experiencing the same degree of burnout, because the work is organized in a way that distributes effort appropriately. When therapists shift into the caretaker role, the work becomes increasingly dependent on the therapist's effort, which leads to the pattern of escalation described earlier.

This is why burnout is not simply a matter of working too much. It is a consequence of working in a role that requires more effort than the system can sustain, and once that role is identified and corrected, the experience of the work begins to change.

CHAPTER 5 — SUMMARY

- Burnout is closely tied to a shift from mentor to caretaker role
- The caretaker role develops when therapy is focused on content instead of theme and process
- In the caretaker role, therapists feel responsible for producing progress each session
- Attempting to resolve individual situations increases pressure and emotional fatigue
- The mentor role focuses on guiding understanding while maintaining appropriate responsibility
- Shifting back to the mentor role redistributes effort and improves sustainability

CHAPTER 6

Hurt vs Harm

As therapists shift from a mentor role into a caretaker role, one of the most common and consequential errors involves how they interpret patient discomfort. When the therapy approach is misaligned, discomfort is often treated as something that should be reduced as quickly as possible, and this creates a subtle but important confusion between two very different experiences: hurt and harm.

Hurt is an expected and often necessary part of psychological change and growth. It emerges when a patient begins to confront patterns that have been avoided, when previously held assumptions are challenged, and when new ways of thinking or behaving create tension with established habits. This type of discomfort is not a sign that something is going wrong, but a signal that something meaningful is being engaged, and when it is handled correctly, it supports the patient's ability to grow.

Harm, by contrast, reflects a movement away from stability and function and prevents growth from occurring. It arises when an intervention overwhelms a patient's capacity to process what is being experienced, when the therapeutic process reinforces maladaptive patterns, or when the patient is pushed beyond what can be integrated in a constructive way. While hurt is associated with forward movement, harm disrupts that movement and reduces the patient's ability to engage in the work.

The difficulty is that, in practice, these experiences can appear similar on the surface. Both involve discomfort, both can include strong emotional reactions, and both can create uncertainty within the session. Without a clear framework for interpreting what is happening, therapists often default to reducing discomfort, assuming that if a patient is distressed, something must be wrong. This assumption is reinforced by a broader cultural belief that if a person feels hurt or uncomfortable, it must mean that they have been treated unfairly or wronged in some way, which can lead both patients and therapists to interpret discomfort as evidence of harm even when no such harm has occurred.

This dynamic was present in the work of the therapist I was supervising. As she became more aware of the underlying theme and the way her patient was interpreting that theme, she also began to notice how often the patient interpreted discomfort as evidence that something had been done to her. When situations did not go as expected or when others responded in ways that felt challenging, the patient would often default to the belief that she had been treated unfairly, which reinforced a sense of victimization and made it more difficult to examine her own role in shaping those interactions. In these moments, the therapist initially felt pulled to reduce that discomfort, because it appeared to signal that something had gone wrong.

Over time, however, it became clear that not all discomfort was the same. There were moments when the patient's reactions reflected an increase in awareness, even though that awareness was uncomfortable, and other moments when the patient became overwhelmed in a way that reduced clarity and made it more difficult to engage in the work. The difference between these experiences was not the presence of discomfort, but whether the discomfort supported growth or prevented it. A temporary increase in distress did not necessarily indicate harm, and in many cases, it was a necessary part of helping the patient recognize patterns that had previously gone unexamined.

This is where the distinction between hurt and harm becomes clinically useful. When discomfort is associated with increased awareness, it often indicates that the therapist is working at the level of theme and process, helping the patient see patterns that were previously outside of conscious awareness. When discomfort is associated with decreased capacity, it suggests that the work has moved beyond what the patient can currently integrate, and that the approach may need to be adjusted. The therapist's role is not to eliminate discomfort, but to understand its function within the process and respond accordingly.

Without this distinction, therapists are likely to respond in ways that unintentionally reinforce the burnout pattern. If all discomfort is treated as something to be avoided, or as evidence that the patient has been wronged, the therapist will consistently move toward reducing distress, which shifts the focus back to content and immediate problem-solving. This not only limits the patient's ability to develop new capacity, but also increases the therapist's responsibility for managing the session, which contributes to the escalation of effort described in earlier chapters.

At the same time, if discomfort is not monitored carefully, it is possible to push a patient into a state where harm occurs. This is why the goal is not to create discomfort, but to recognize when discomfort is serving a constructive function and when it is not. The therapist must maintain a level of engagement that allows the patient to remain connected to the work while still being challenged by it, which requires both awareness of the underlying structure and careful attention to the patient's capacity.

The therapist I was supervising began to apply this distinction as she became more comfortable working at the level of theme and process. Instead of measuring her effectiveness by how quickly she could reduce discomfort or resolve individual situations, she began to pay closer attention to whether the patient was developing a clearer understanding of the patterns shaping her experience. When discomfort arose in those moments, she was less likely to move away from it, because she could see that it was connected to growth rather than to harm.

This shift reduced the pressure to stabilize every emotional reaction and allowed the work to remain focused on what was most important. Instead of attempting to manage the patient's experience in real time, the therapist was able to guide the process in a way that supported both understanding and capacity, which in turn reduced the amount of effort required to maintain progress.

The distinction between hurt and harm reinforces the difference between the mentor and caretaker roles. The caretaker moves quickly to reduce discomfort, often at the expense of long-term change, while the mentor maintains enough stability for the patient to engage with the work while allowing discomfort that supports growth to remain present. This difference in approach has a direct impact on both the patient's development and the therapist's experience of the work.

When therapists consistently confuse hurt with harm, they are more likely to remain in the caretaker role, increase their level of effort, and contribute to the burnout pattern. When they are able to distinguish between the two, they can maintain a more effective role, support meaningful change, and reduce the likelihood of burnout developing over time.

CHAPTER 6 — SUMMARY

- Hurt is a necessary part of growth and reflects increased awareness
- Harm disrupts stability and prevents growth
- Discomfort does not automatically indicate that harm has occurred
- Patients and therapists may misinterpret hurt as evidence of being wronged
- Reducing all discomfort reinforces the caretaker role and limits progress
- Distinguishing hurt from harm supports effective therapy and reduces burnout

CHAPTER 7

Content vs Process

You have already been introduced to the distinction between content and process, and at a conceptual level it may seem straightforward. However, understanding the distinction is not the same as being able to recognize it in real time, particularly in the middle of a session where multiple details are competing for your attention. In this chapter, we will return to this concept in greater depth, not to repeat it, but to make it familiar enough that you can begin to see it clearly as it is happening and apply it in a way that changes how the work feels.

One of the most common and costly errors therapists make is focusing on the content of a patient's experience rather than on the process through which that experience is organized and understood. This distinction is often described conceptually, but in practice it becomes one of the primary factors that determines whether therapy is effective and sustainable or confusing and overwhelming.

Content refers to the individual details of a patient's life, including the events, situations, and interactions that are described in session. These details are often emotionally charged and feel immediately relevant, which naturally draws the therapist's attention toward them. When a patient describes conflict with a family member, frustration at work, or distress related to a recent event, the therapist is presented with information that appears to require understanding and response, and it is reasonable to begin by engaging with that material.

The challenge is that content, by itself, does not organize. Each new situation introduces additional variables, and without a framework for understanding how those situations are connected, the therapist is required to engage with each one independently. Over time, this creates an expanding field of information that becomes increasingly difficult to manage, particularly when multiple emotionally significant issues are present at the same time.

Process, by contrast, refers to how the patient is interpreting and responding to the underlying theme that organizes those experiences. While content changes from situation to situation, the way the patient interprets those situations tends to remain consistent. It is this consistency that allows the therapist to move beyond individual problems and begin to understand the pattern that is shaping the patient's experience.

The therapist I was supervising encountered this distinction as she continued to review her sessions. Initially, her attention was drawn almost entirely to content, as each situation felt important and required a response. As she attempted to track these details and generate solutions, the complexity of the work increased, and the sense of overwhelm followed. What began to change was not the content itself, but her ability to shift attention toward the process through which the patient was interpreting that content.

As she became more aware of the patient's underlying theme and the way that theme was being interpreted, she began to recognize that many of the situations being described were variations of the same pattern. Instead of seeing each problem as something new, she began to see each one as another expression of the same organizing structure. This shift did not eliminate the content, but it changed how that content was understood.

This is where the distinction becomes clinically useful. When therapy is focused on content, the therapist is required to respond to each situation individually, which increases cognitive load and reinforces the need for ongoing effort. When therapy is focused on process, the therapist is able to recognize patterns across situations, which reduces the number of unique problems that need to be addressed and allows the work to become more efficient.

This does not mean that content is ignored. Content provides the information necessary to identify the underlying theme and the way that theme is being interpreted, and it remains an essential part of the work. The difference is that content is no longer treated as the primary target of intervention, but as evidence that supports a deeper understanding of the patient's experience.

The therapist I was supervising began to apply this shift in a practical way. Instead of attempting to resolve each situation as it arose, she began selecting the most useful moments within the session that most clearly reflected the underlying pattern and using those moments to help the patient see how the same process was occurring across different contexts.

As a result, the patient was able to recognize patterns that had previously felt unrelated, and the work began to feel more coherent and more manageable.

This shift also changed how the patient experienced the work. When therapy is focused on content, the patient often experiences each session as a response to the most recent problem, which can create the sense that progress is dependent on resolving individual situations. When therapy is focused on process, the patient begins to understand how those situations are connected, which allows progress to occur at the level of pattern rather than at the level of individual events.

Without this distinction, therapists are likely to remain in the caretaker role, responding to each situation as it appears and attempting to manage the patient's experience in real time. This reinforces the burnout pattern, because responsibility continues to shift toward the therapist, effort continues to increase, and the work becomes more difficult to sustain.

With this distinction, therapists are able to maintain the mentor role, guiding the patient toward an understanding of the underlying theme and the way that theme is being interpreted. This allows responsibility to be appropriately distributed, reduces unnecessary effort, and creates a structure that supports both effectiveness and sustainability.

The difference between content and process is not simply a theoretical concept. It is a practical distinction that determines how therapy is conducted, how progress is achieved, and how sustainable the work becomes over time. When therapists are able to consistently recognize and work at the level of process, the complexity of the work decreases, the need for excessive effort is reduced, and the likelihood of burnout is significantly diminished.

CHAPTER 7 — SUMMARY

- Content consists of the individual details of a patient's experience
- Process reflects how those experiences are interpreted
- Theme and process together organize all content
- Content alone creates increasing complexity and overwhelm
- Focusing on process allows patterns to be recognized across situations
- Process-focused work reduces effort and improves sustainability

CHAPTER 8

Why Therapists Work Harder Than Patients

One of the clearest indicators that the therapy approach has become inefficient is a shift in effort, where the therapist begins working harder than the patient. This shift is not always obvious at first, because it develops gradually as the therapist attempts to manage increasing complexity within the session, but over time it becomes one of the most reliable signs that the work is no longer organized in a way that can be sustained.

In an effective therapeutic process, effort is distributed in a way that reflects the roles of both the therapist and the patient. The therapist provides structure, identifies patterns, and guides understanding, while the patient engages with that understanding and applies it to their life outside of the session. When this balance is maintained, the work progresses in a way that is both effective and sustainable, because responsibility remains appropriately shared.

When the therapy approach becomes misaligned, this balance begins to shift. As described in previous chapters, when theme and process are not clearly identified, the therapist is left working at the level of content, which requires responding to each situation individually. As the number of situations increases, the therapist becomes responsible for tracking details, maintaining continuity, and generating responses, which leads to an increase in effort that is not matched by an increase in effectiveness.

The therapist I was supervising began to notice this shift in her own work. As sessions became more complex, she found herself thinking more about her patients outside of the session, reviewing details, replaying conversations, and trying to determine what should be addressed next. During the session, she felt a growing pressure to keep the conversation moving, to identify something useful, and to ensure that progress was being made. Over time, this created a sense that she was carrying the work, rather than guiding it.

This is how the imbalance develops. The therapist begins to invest more time, more cognitive effort, and more emotional energy into each case, while the patient's role in the process becomes less defined. Instead of being responsible for applying insight and making changes outside of the session, the patient begins to rely more heavily on the therapist to generate direction and maintain progress. As this continues, the therapist becomes the primary driver of the work, and the system begins to break down.

One of the reasons this shift is difficult to recognize is that it often feels like the therapist is doing a better job. Working harder, thinking more, and investing more effort can feel like increased dedication, and in the absence of a clear framework, it is easy to assume that this level of effort is necessary. However, when effort increases without a corresponding increase in effectiveness, it is a sign that the system is not functioning correctly.

This dynamic is reinforced when progress is defined in terms of resolving individual situations. If the therapist believes that success depends on addressing specific problems within each session, then increased effort becomes the primary tool for achieving that goal. As a result, the therapist feels responsible for producing outcomes that are not entirely within their control, which leads to increased pressure and a greater likelihood of burnout.

The therapist I was supervising experienced this directly. She began to feel that if a session ended without resolving at least one issue, she had not done her job effectively, which created a persistent sense of pressure to produce results. This led her to invest more effort into trying to control the direction of the session, often working harder to solve problems than the patient was working to understand them. Over time, this imbalance made the work feel increasingly unsustainable.

When viewed through the lens of theme and process, this imbalance becomes easier to understand. If the therapist is working at the level of content, each situation requires attention, and the number of situations can easily exceed what can be managed effectively. If the therapist is working at the level of process, the number of unique problems is reduced, because multiple situations can be understood within a single framework. This shift naturally redistributes effort, because the therapist is no longer responsible for solving each problem individually.

This is why the question of effort is so important. In an effective system, the patient should be working at least as hard as the therapist, and often harder, because the patient is the one applying the work in their daily life.

The Burnout Pattern

When the therapist is working harder than the patient, it indicates that responsibility has shifted in a way that is not sustainable, and that the therapy approach needs to be adjusted.

Recognizing this imbalance allows the therapist to make a critical correction. Instead of increasing effort, the therapist can shift focus back to identifying the underlying theme and the way that theme is being interpreted, which reduces the number of problems that need to be managed and clarifies where effort should be applied. As this happens, the therapist's role becomes more defined, the patient's role becomes more active, and the work begins to feel more manageable.

This is not a matter of working less, but of working correctly. When effort is aligned with an effective structure, the same amount of work produces better results with less strain. When effort is misaligned, even a smaller amount of work can feel overwhelming, because the system itself is not functioning in a way that supports progress.

CHAPTER 8 — SUMMARY

- When therapists work harder than patients, the system is inefficient
- Content-focused therapy shifts effort and responsibility toward the therapist
- Increased effort without improved outcomes signals structural misalignment
- Defining success as resolving situations increases pressure and burnout
- Process-focused work redistributes effort and improves sustainability

CHAPTER 9

Correcting the Pattern

By the time the burnout pattern is recognized, the therapist is often already aware that something in the work is not functioning the way it should. The sessions feel heavier than expected, the effort required to maintain progress continues to increase, and there is a growing sense that the work is being carried rather than guided. What is less clear at this stage is how to change it, because the habits that created the pattern are the same habits the therapist has relied on to try to solve it.

The therapist I was supervising reached this point gradually. After recognizing that the problem was not simply the number of sessions, she began to notice how often her attention was pulled toward the details of each situation, even when she knew that focusing on those details was contributing to her sense of overwhelm. In session, this pull felt automatic. When a patient introduced a new problem, the instinct to understand it, respond to it, and move it toward resolution was immediate, and stepping away from that instinct felt, at first, like she was not doing her job.

The first attempts to shift away from this pattern were not clean or consistent. There were moments in which she would recognize the underlying theme and begin to move the conversation in that direction, only to feel the urge to return to the details when the patient became distressed or when the conversation seemed to lose direction. At times, this created a sense of uncertainty, as if she were allowing something important to go unaddressed, and the instinct to regain control by focusing on content would re-emerge.

This hesitation is a normal part of the correction process. When a therapist has been working at the level of content, the absence of that familiar structure can feel disorienting, and the initial shift toward theme and process does not immediately produce the same sense of control. Instead, it often requires the therapist to tolerate a temporary increase in uncertainty while learning to trust a different way of organizing the work.

Over time, the shift becomes more recognizable. Instead of following each new situation into a detailed analysis, the therapist begins to notice when the same pattern is appearing in different forms and allows the conversation to move in that direction. This does not mean ignoring the patient's experience, but rather using the content selectively to highlight the pattern that is already present. The work becomes less about solving each problem and more about helping the patient see what is generating those problems.

There are moments in this process where the therapist must make a decision that feels counterintuitive. A patient may introduce a situation that appears urgent or emotionally charged, and the instinct is to respond directly to that situation. Instead, the therapist may choose to pause and reflect something about the pattern that is emerging, even if that means not immediately addressing the specific problem that was presented. In these moments, the therapist is not avoiding the work, but redirecting it toward the level at which change is actually possible.

This shift often changes how the patient responds. When the therapist remains focused on content, the patient may continue to bring in new situations, expecting each one to be addressed individually. When the therapist begins to highlight patterns, the patient may initially experience confusion or even mild frustration, particularly if they are accustomed to having each problem approached directly. However, as the pattern becomes clearer, the patient begins to recognize connections that were previously invisible, and the work starts to feel more coherent.

The therapist I was supervising experienced this progression in a very real way. There were sessions in which she felt the pull to return to content and had to consciously choose to stay with the pattern she was beginning to see. There were also moments where she moved too quickly or pushed the patient beyond what could be integrated, and she had to adjust her approach to maintain engagement without overwhelming the patient. These adjustments were not signs of failure, but part of developing the ability to work at a different level.

As this process continued, the internal experience of the work began to change. The urgency to resolve each situation decreased, the pressure to produce immediate outcomes lessened, and the sense of carrying the work began to diminish. Instead of feeling responsible for what happened in each session, she began to see her role as guiding the patient toward an understanding that could be applied across situations, which allowed the work to feel more stable and more sustainable.

This is how the burnout pattern is corrected. It is not a single decision or a single intervention, but a gradual shift in how the therapist engages with the work. The habits that reinforce the pattern are replaced with habits that interrupt it, and over time the system begins to function differently. The therapist is no longer relying on increasing effort to maintain progress, and the work begins to organize itself in a way that supports both effectiveness and sustainability.

This process does not eliminate difficulty, but it changes the nature of that difficulty. Instead of struggling to keep up with an expanding set of problems, the therapist is learning to see and work with patterns that remain consistent across situations. As this ability develops, the work becomes less reactive, more intentional, and more aligned with how change actually occurs.

Correcting the pattern, then, is not about doing less. It is about working differently, and that difference becomes most apparent in the moment when the therapist chooses to move away from what is immediately visible and toward what is consistently present.

CHAPTER 9 — SUMMARY

- Correcting burnout requires changing how the therapist engages in real time
- Shifting away from content initially feels uncertain and counterintuitive
- Therapists often feel pulled back into old patterns during early correction
- Working at the level of pattern reduces pressure to resolve each situation
- Progress becomes more stable as the therapist develops consistency in approach
- Burnout is reduced as effort becomes aligned with an effective structure

CHAPTER 10

How Therapists Learn to See This

By this point, the structure of the work should be clear. The difference between focusing on content and working at the level of theme and process has been described, and the impact of that difference on both effectiveness and burnout has been established. What is not yet clear is how a therapist develops the ability to see and apply this in real time, because understanding the concept is not the same as being able to use it consistently in practice.

This is where many therapists begin to feel uncertain. The distinction between content and process may make sense when reading it, and the examples may feel familiar, but when sitting in a session with a patient who is describing multiple emotionally charged situations, the same sense of overwhelm can return. The details feel immediate, the pressure to respond remains, and the ability to identify the underlying theme may not be as clear as it seemed when reading about it.

This is not a failure of understanding, but a reflection of how this skill develops. Seeing theme and process is not something that emerges simply by being introduced to the concept. It is a form of pattern recognition that develops over time, and like other forms of complex recognition, it requires repeated exposure, guided correction, and the ability to observe the work from a perspective that is difficult to maintain while actively participating in it.

The therapist I was supervising experienced this directly. Even after she began to understand the concept, there were many sessions in which she struggled to identify the underlying theme in real time. She would often recognize it after the session had ended or when reviewing the work in supervision, but during the session itself, the pull toward content remained strong. This created a temporary gap between what she understood and what she could consistently apply.

This gap is expected. When a therapist has been trained to focus on content, that pattern becomes automatic, and shifting away from it requires the development of a new way of organizing information. In the early stages, this often means that the therapist will move back and forth between content and process, sometimes recognizing the pattern clearly and at other times losing it as the session unfolds.

This was not how I initially learned to see this. I did not have a supervisor who could consistently point out the underlying theme and the way it was being interpreted in real time, and because of that, the process of learning to see it was much slower and far less direct. Much of it came from repeatedly reviewing my own sessions and trying to understand why certain interactions felt effective while others did not.

Over time, I developed a way of organizing what I was observing that allowed me to begin identifying patterns more consistently. I would watch recordings of my sessions and start by writing down as many of the content details as I could identify, focusing on the specific situations, interactions, and events the patient described. Once those details were on paper, I would then attempt to identify the different ways the patient seemed to be interpreting those situations, noting recurring patterns in how they made sense of what was happening. Only after doing that would I attempt to identify a theme that could account for all of those details and interpretations at once.

This process was not efficient, and it required a significant amount of time and repetition before it began to produce consistent results. There were many instances where the theme I identified did not fully account for the content, or where the patterns I thought I saw were incomplete or inaccurate. However, over time, as the same patterns began to appear across different patients and different sessions, the distinction between content, process, and theme became easier to recognize, and what initially required deliberate effort began to occur more naturally.

The therapist I was supervising had a very different experience. Instead of having to work through this process independently, she was able to review sessions in a structured way and receive direct feedback about what was being missed and what was being seen correctly. As we continued this process, there were sessions where she would attempt to identify the theme and the process on her own, followed by a comparison to what I was seeing, and over time the gap between those two perspectives began to close. What had initially felt difficult to recognize became more apparent, and the need for external guidance decreased as her ability to see patterns in real time improved.

As this process continued, the development of the skill followed a recognizable progression. In the early stages, patterns were identified only after the session had ended, often with the help of supervision or reflection. As exposure increased, those patterns began to emerge more quickly, sometimes just after they occurred and eventually while the session was still unfolding. The content continued to draw attention, but it no longer dominated it completely, and the therapist became able to move between the details of the situation and the structure beneath it.

With continued practice and feedback, the skill becomes more stable. The therapist begins to recognize patterns as they are forming, and instead of being led by the content, they are able to guide the session based on the underlying structure. The work becomes more organized, not because the problems are simpler, but because the therapist is no longer trying to manage every detail independently. What once required deliberate effort becomes more automatic, and the therapist is able to maintain clarity without the same level of cognitive strain.

This progression does not occur automatically, and it cannot be developed in isolation. Supervision plays a critical role, because therapists are limited in their ability to see their own blind spots, particularly in real time. When reviewing their own sessions, therapists often focus on what they intended to do rather than what actually occurred, and without external feedback, important patterns may be missed repeatedly. When the actual interaction is reviewed, however, the work can be examined in detail, allowing patterns to be identified, missed moments to be recognized, and attention to be redirected more effectively.

Another factor that influences this development is depth of training. Therapists who are exposed to multiple modalities without developing depth in any one framework often struggle to organize what they are observing, because there is no stable structure through which patterns can be consistently interpreted. In contrast, therapists who develop depth within a coherent model are better able to recognize patterns, because they have a framework that allows them to organize information across situations.

This is why the purpose of this book is not to teach every aspect of this skill, but to make the structure of the work visible so that therapists know what they are looking for. Once the structure is clear, the process of developing the skill becomes more directed, and therapists are better able to recognize when they are working at the appropriate level and when they have been pulled back into content.

Understanding this progression is important, because it prevents therapists from misinterpreting the difficulty of the skill as a sign that something is wrong. The challenge is not a failure of ability, but a reflection of the level of development required to perform the work at a high level. When this is recognized, therapists are able to approach the learning process with greater clarity and less frustration, which allows the skill to develop more effectively over time.

CHAPTER 10 — SUMMARY

- Recognizing theme and process is a learned skill that develops over time
- Understanding the concept does not guarantee real-time application
- Early development involves moving between content and process
- Pattern recognition improves with repetition, supervision, and feedback
- The skill progresses from delayed recognition to real-time clarity
- Depth of training supports consistent pattern recognition

CHAPTER 11

Structuring Therapy Correctly

Understanding the correct role of the therapist and the importance of working at the level of theme and process is necessary, but it is not sufficient on its own. Even when therapists are clear about what they are trying to do, they can still become overwhelmed if the session itself is not organized in a way that supports that clarity. When there is no consistent structure guiding the work, the therapist is forced to make continuous decisions about what matters, what to prioritize, and how to proceed, and over time that decision-making process becomes one of the primary sources of cognitive strain.

Without structure, even a therapist who understands the model will drift. The session may begin with a clear intention to maintain focus on theme and process, but as new details are introduced, attention is gradually pulled back toward content. The therapist begins responding to what is most immediate rather than what is most important, and as the session becomes more reactive, it also becomes heavier. This drift is not a failure of understanding, but a predictable outcome of working without a framework that consistently organizes the interaction.

The therapist I was supervising experienced this directly as she began to improve her ability to recognize patterns. There were sessions where she could clearly see the underlying theme, but without a structure to guide the session, she would still find herself pulled into extended discussions of individual situations. Afterward, she could recognize that the work had drifted, but in the moment, there was no consistent framework to help her redirect the conversation efficiently.

Most therapists are taught techniques before they are taught structure. They learn how to validate, reflect, and respond to different types of patient presentations, but those skills are often applied in response to whatever the patient presents in the moment. Without a consistent structure, therapy becomes a series of reactions rather than a guided process, and the therapist is required to generate direction in real time. That constant adjustment increases cognitive load and contributes directly to burnout.

Structure changes this completely. When therapy is organized within a consistent framework, the therapist is no longer deciding from scratch what to do at each moment. The session still requires attention and flexibility, but the overall direction is established, which reduces the number of decisions that need to be made. This allows the therapist to focus more on recognizing patterns and less on managing the flow of the conversation.

One example of this type of structure is a therapy flow. While the specific language may vary depending on the modality being used, the underlying progression serves the same function. The session begins with establishing a clear frame and shared expectations, allowing both the therapist and the patient to understand their roles. The patient is then given space to describe what has been happening, providing the content necessary to identify patterns while expressing their experience.

From there, the work moves into validation, not as an endpoint, but as a way to accurately recognize the patient's experience so that the underlying theme can be identified. Once sufficient information has been gathered, the focus shifts toward understanding what is happening beneath the surface, including recognizing the pattern, identifying how it is maintained, and helping the patient see their role within it.

As this becomes clearer, the patient is guided toward accepting the reality of the situation and the consequences that follow from it. This stage often involves discomfort, but as described in the previous chapter, that discomfort can represent growth rather than harm when it is handled correctly. From there, the work moves toward developing new responses and helping the patient apply those responses outside of the session.

The session then moves toward a clear ending, where the patient leaves with an understanding of what they are working on and how they will apply it. This provides closure to the session and prevents the therapist from carrying unresolved content forward.

The specific sequence is less important than the function it serves. Structure prevents the therapist from remaining in content, from stopping at validation, and from moving prematurely into problem-solving. It ensures that the work progresses from understanding to insight and from insight to action, which reduces the need for the therapist to compensate with additional effort.

Without this type of structure, the therapist must rely on intuition to guide the session, deciding in real time what is most important and what should be addressed next. This creates constant decision-making pressure, which becomes mentally exhausting over time. With structure, many of those decisions are already embedded in the process, allowing the therapist to focus on recognizing patterns rather than generating direction.

Another critical function of structure is that it clarifies responsibility. When the session is organized around a consistent framework, it becomes clear what belongs to the therapist and what belongs to the patient. The therapist is responsible for guiding the process and identifying patterns, while the patient is responsible for applying that understanding outside of the session. This clarity prevents the gradual shift into the caretaker role and protects against the accumulation of unnecessary effort.

The therapist I was supervising began to notice that as she relied more on a consistent structure, she felt less pressure to control the session. Instead of trying to ensure that each problem was resolved, she focused on moving the work through the structure, which naturally brought the session to the level of pattern and understanding. This reduced the sense of urgency she had previously experienced and made it easier to maintain the mentor role.

Structure does not mean rigidity. Sessions will not always follow a perfect sequence, and patients may move between different parts of the process at different speeds. Structure is not about forcing the session into a fixed format, but about ensuring that the essential components of the work are present so that the therapist does not compensate for missing elements with increased effort.

When structure is in place, the therapist no longer feels lost during sessions, because there is a clear sense of direction. The therapist can recognize when the session is staying in content for too long, when a pattern has been identified but not developed, and when the work needs to move toward application. This reduces uncertainty, and as uncertainty decreases, cognitive strain decreases as well.

At the same time, the patient experiences the work differently. Instead of leaving with a general sense of understanding, the patient leaves with clarity about what they need to do. The connection between insight and behavior becomes more direct, and the patient takes a more active role in the process. This is where structure begins to directly reduce burnout.

The therapist is no longer carrying the session through effort alone. The structure of the work supports clarity, distributes responsibility appropriately, and reduces the need for constant adjustment. The work becomes more efficient, not because less is being done, but because the right things are being done in the right order.

Ultimately, structure is what allows everything else in this model to function. It supports the mentor role by maintaining clear boundaries around responsibility, supports process-based work by ensuring that the session moves beyond content, and supports the development of patient capacity by connecting insight to action. Without structure, even the best understanding will drift into inefficiency. With structure, the work becomes sustainable.

CHAPTER 11 — SUMMARY

- Structure reduces cognitive load by organizing the session
- Without structure, therapists drift back into content and reactivity
- Structure allows therapists to focus on patterns instead of managing flow
- A consistent therapy flow supports insight, application, and closure
- Structure clarifies responsibility and protects against the caretaker role
- When structure is present, the work becomes more efficient and sustainable

CHAPTER 12

Fixing Burnout in Real Time

By the time burnout is recognized, the pattern that produces it is often already in motion. The therapist is working harder than the patient, focusing on content rather than process, and carrying responsibility that does not belong to them. At that point, reducing workload may provide temporary relief, but it does not address the underlying structure that is creating the problem. A more effective approach is to intervene earlier, because burnout does not begin at the level of weeks or months but within individual sessions, often in subtle moments that are easy to overlook.

These moments are rarely obvious when they occur. They often begin as a shift in attention, where the therapist feels pulled toward the details of a situation and begins to follow the content rather than observing the pattern that is emerging. This shift is frequently accompanied by a sense of urgency, as though something needs to be solved immediately, and it can create the impression that the therapist is being responsive and engaged when in reality the work is beginning to drift.

The therapist I was supervising began to recognize these moments as her awareness increased. There were points in sessions where she could feel herself becoming more invested in understanding exactly what had happened, why it had happened, and what should be done next, and in those moments the pressure to produce an answer would increase. Initially, she would follow the instinct to determine what should be done next, focusing on how to respond to the situation in order to move it toward resolution. While her effort to understand what had happened and why it had happened was appropriate and necessary, the moment she shifted into deciding what should be done next, the session began to move away from the underlying pattern and into the details of the situation. This shift limited her ability to see how the situation reflected a broader theme and instead narrowed the work to a single instance, which increased the likelihood that she would take on responsibility for generating the outcome rather than helping the patient understand how that outcome could be produced differently.

Recognizing this shift is the first step in correcting it. Instead of continuing to follow the content, the therapist can pause and redirect attention toward the pattern, shifting the question from what happened to what is repeating. This does not require ignoring the patient's experience, but it changes how that experience is used, because the details become evidence of the pattern rather than the primary focus of the work.

At the same time, the therapist must re-establish the correct role. When drift occurs, the therapist often begins to relate more personally to the patient's experience, and as that identification increases, so does the sense of responsibility for resolving the situation. This is one of the clearest indicators that the therapist is moving from the mentor role into the caretaker role, because instead of observing the pattern, the therapist begins to participate in it. Correcting this requires a conscious return to the mentor role, where the focus remains on helping the patient understand what is happening and develop the capacity to respond differently, rather than attempting to control the outcome.

Discomfort is often where this shift becomes most visible. When the therapist feels the urge to reduce the patient's pain, it is usually a signal that they are moving into the caretaker role, and at that point the distinction between hurt and harm becomes essential. If the discomfort is part of the growth process, it should not be removed but understood and used. Allowing discomfort to remain while helping the patient understand what to do with it returns the session to a developmental framework and removes the therapist's responsibility for managing the patient's emotional state.

As this happens, responsibility begins to return to the patient. When burnout is developing, responsibility has usually shifted toward the therapist, who is thinking more, analyzing more, and attempting to guide the outcome more directly. Reversing this requires that the therapist ensure the patient leaves with a clear understanding of what they need to do and how they will apply the work outside of the session, which restores the balance of effort and reduces the burden on the therapist.

Another important part of this correction is simplification. When therapists feel overwhelmed, it is often because they are trying to manage too many variables at once, and as the details expand and the possibilities multiply, the session begins to feel disorganized. Returning to the core pattern restores clarity, because the therapist does not need to address every detail but to understand what is repeating and what needs to change, which organizes complexity rather than ignoring it.

The therapist I was supervising began to apply these corrections more consistently over time. There were moments where she would feel the familiar pull toward content and recognize it more quickly, allowing her to redirect the session before it became fully disorganized. These corrections were not dramatic, but they were cumulative, and as they accumulated, the overall structure of her sessions began to stabilize. As this process became more consistent, she also began to notice a change in her patients. Situations that previously seemed to repeat without resolution began to produce different outcomes, not because each situation was being solved individually, but because the patient was beginning to recognize the pattern that was generating them. Instead of returning each week with variations of the same problem, patients started to demonstrate increased awareness and make more meaningful changes outside of the session, which reinforced the shift away from content and toward process as the primary focus of the work.

The therapist must also learn to leave the session clean. When the structure is correct, the work of the session is complete once the pattern has been identified, the patient understands their role, and there is a clear next step. If the therapist leaves still trying to solve the patient's life, the boundary of responsibility has not been maintained, and the pattern continues beyond the session.

Over time, these real-time corrections change the trajectory of the work. Each time the therapist recognizes drift and returns to structure, the session becomes more efficient. Each time responsibility is placed correctly, the imbalance decreases. Each time the therapist focuses on process instead of content, cognitive load is reduced, and as the structure becomes more consistent, burnout begins to decrease as well.

Burnout is not controlled by reducing the number of sessions. It is controlled by correcting what happens within each session.

CHAPTER 12 — SUMMARY

- Burnout begins within individual sessions, not just over time
- Drift occurs when attention shifts from pattern to content
- Understanding content is necessary, but treating it as the target creates inefficiency
- Recognizing drift allows for immediate correction
- Returning to the mentor role restores proper responsibility
- Repeated real-time corrections reduce burnout and improve patient outcomes

CHAPTER 13

Documentation and Thinking

For many therapists, the work does not end when the session ends. After the patient leaves, there is still documentation to complete, notes to write, and the responsibility of translating the session into a record that accurately reflects what occurred. For some therapists, this process is relatively quick and manageable. For others, it becomes one of the most exhausting parts of their day, often carrying as much cognitive weight as the sessions themselves.

This difference is not primarily about time, but about how the therapist is thinking, because documentation is not separate from therapy. It is a continuation of it. The way a therapist understands the session determines how they document it, and the way they document it reflects the level at which they are working. When the thinking is disorganized, the documentation becomes heavy. When the thinking is clear, the documentation becomes efficient.

When therapy is content-focused, documentation follows the same pattern. The therapist feels responsible for capturing everything that happened, including each event, each interaction, and each detail of the patient's experience. The note becomes a narrative that attempts to recreate the session in full, which requires the therapist to hold and organize a large amount of information long after the session has ended. As this process repeats throughout the day, the cognitive demand accumulates, making the work feel heavier with each additional patient.

The weight of documentation in this case is not coming from the act of writing itself, but from the effort required to manage the information. The therapist is not only documenting the session, but continuing to carry it forward by replaying details and attempting to ensure that nothing important is missed, which extends the cognitive load of the session beyond its natural endpoint.

The therapist I was supervising began to recognize this pattern in her own work. Early on, her notes reflected the same content-driven approach she was using in session, and she found herself trying to include every detail in order to feel confident that the documentation was complete. This often required her to mentally revisit the session, replaying what had been said and trying to determine what was important enough to include. Over time, this made documentation feel like an extension of the session rather than a conclusion of it.

As her thinking shifted, her documentation began to change as well. Instead of attempting to capture every detail, she began focusing on the underlying pattern that defined the session, identifying how the patient had responded to that pattern and what needed to happen next. The note became less about recreating the conversation and more about clarifying the structure of the work, which reduced the amount of information she needed to hold and allowed her to complete documentation more efficiently. In many cases, this shift reduced the time required for documentation by half or more, while at the same time improving the clarity and usefulness of the notes, because they were more focused, more precise, and more aligned with what actually mattered in the session.

A common complaint among therapists is that the work extends well beyond the last session of the day, because documentation accumulates and must be completed afterward. It often feels as though the therapist is working a second shift, first seeing patients and then writing notes for each session once the day has ended. As the number of sessions increases, this backlog can become one of the most exhausting parts of the work.

As the therapist I was supervising became more consistent in organizing her thinking around theme and process, this pattern changed. Instead of allowing documentation to accumulate, she was able to complete each note during the time between sessions. Because the structure of the work was clear, each note could be written quickly, often in just a few minutes, focusing on the theme, the way the patient was interpreting that theme, and a small number of content examples to support it. By the end of the day, there was no backlog of notes to complete, and the final session required only a brief period of documentation before the workday was finished.

This shift did not reduce the quality of the documentation. If anything, it improved it. The notes became more targeted, more precise, and more useful, because they reflected the structure of the work rather than attempting to capture every detail. At the same time, the overall experience of the work changed, because the therapist was no longer carrying the cognitive load of multiple sessions into the end of the day.

This shift improves not only efficiency but also accuracy. When documentation is content-driven, the volume of information increases the likelihood that important elements will be obscured by detail, and the therapist may struggle to identify what actually matters. When documentation is organized around pattern and process, the structure clarifies the information, making it easier to identify the key elements of the session without relying on excessive detail.

This is why documentation becomes such a significant contributor to burnout when it is content-driven. The therapist is not only working during the session, but continuing to work afterward, organizing and reprocessing information that was never structured clearly in the first place. Over time, this creates a cumulative burden that can make even a moderate caseload feel overwhelming.

In contrast, when documentation is aligned with process, each session has a natural endpoint. The pattern has been identified, the patient understands their role, and the next step is clear, which allows the therapist to document the session efficiently and move on without carrying unnecessary detail forward. This containment reduces cognitive fatigue and allows the therapist to maintain clarity across multiple sessions.

The difference becomes more noticeable over the course of a day. When each session produces a detailed narrative that must be remembered and recorded, the therapist's mental load continues to increase, and by the end of the day the exhaustion is not only the result of the sessions themselves, but of the accumulated effort required to manage and document them. When each session is organized around process, the work remains contained, allowing the therapist to complete the session, document the essential elements, and move on with less residual cognitive strain.

This is another example of how burnout is reinforced outside of the session as well as within it, because when therapists carry content into their documentation, they extend the life of the session beyond its natural boundary. When they organize the work around process, they allow the session to end when it is complete.

Understanding this connection changes how documentation is approached, because it is no longer seen as a separate administrative task, but as an extension of clinical thinking. The more organized the thinking, the more efficient the documentation becomes, while the more the therapist focuses on content, the heavier both the session and the documentation will feel.

Ultimately, documentation reflects how the therapist is working. When the therapist is operating at the level of process, the note becomes a clear and concise representation of the work. When the therapist is operating at the level of content, the note becomes an attempt to manage an unstructured set of details, and the difference is not in how much is written, but in how the work is understood.

CHAPTER 13 — SUMMARY

- Burnout begins within individual sessions, not just over time
- Drift occurs when attention shifts from pattern to content
- Understanding content is necessary, but treating it as the target creates inefficiency
- Recognizing drift allows for immediate correction
- Returning to the mentor role restores proper responsibility
- Repeated real-time corrections reduce burnout and improve patient outcomes

CHAPTER 14

Why Therapists Are Not Trained for This

By this point, the structure of the problem should be clear, because burnout is not simply the result of working too much, caring too much, or being exposed to too much emotional intensity. It develops when the therapist is working without a structure that supports clarity, efficiency, and appropriate responsibility, and once this is understood, an important question naturally follows: if this model is so central to both effectiveness and sustainability, why are so many therapists not trained to work this way? The answer is not that therapists are unmotivated or incapable, but that most training systems are not designed to develop this level of skill.

Therapists are introduced to clinical work through a combination of theoretical education and limited practical exposure, where they learn concepts, become familiar with different modalities, and begin seeing patients under supervision. This stage is necessary, but it represents an introduction to the work rather than full immersion in the demands of sustained clinical practice. When therapists transition into full-time work, the environment changes quickly. The number of patients increases, the time between sessions decreases, and the expectation to function independently becomes immediate. During this transition, it is common to experience fatigue, cognitive strain, and early signs of overwhelm, which are often interpreted as evidence that the work itself is inherently unsustainable. In reality, this stage frequently reflects a gap between the demands of the work and the level of skill that has been developed.

The core of that gap is not knowledge, but pattern recognition under pressure. Therapists are often taught how to understand behavior and how to respond to it within individual situations, but they are not consistently trained to identify the underlying theme and the way that theme is being interpreted across multiple situations in real time. Without that ability, the work remains anchored in content, and each new situation feels like a separate problem that must be managed independently. This limitation is not always obvious, because it can be masked by the use of broad or imprecise language. Therapists may describe a case in terms of trauma, control, or other general concepts that appear to organize the patient's experience, but these labels do not always function as true themes, because a useful theme must account for patterns across situations and provide a structure that allows those situations to be understood consistently. When that level of precision is not present, the work continues to rely on content, even when it appears to be conceptually organized.

Another factor that contributes to this gap is how training is structured. Most programs emphasize exposure to multiple modalities, each with its own techniques and conceptual framework, but do not consistently develop depth within a single organizing structure. Without that depth, therapists may have a wide range of tools but no stable framework for deciding when and how to apply them, which increases reliance on intuition and requires therapists to make decisions in real time without a consistent structure to guide them. Supervision, while essential, does not always address this problem, because when supervision is based primarily on the therapist's description of the session, it is limited by the therapist's current perception, and important details may be missed or interpreted inaccurately. Without direct observation of the work, the supervisor is often working with a filtered version of the session, which reduces the ability to identify patterns and provide precise correction.

When supervision includes direct observation, particularly through recorded sessions, the learning process changes. The interaction can be examined in detail, allowing both therapist and supervisor to see where attention shifted, where patterns were missed, and how the session could have been organized differently. This type of feedback develops pattern recognition more effectively, because it is grounded in what actually occurred rather than what is remembered. At the same time, time remains a limiting factor, because developing the ability to consistently recognize theme and process requires repeated exposure across many sessions and many patients. In training environments where clinical hours and supervision are limited, there is often not enough repetition to fully develop this skill before therapists are expected to function independently, which does not make the training ineffective but does mean that it is incomplete.

This distinction becomes clearer when comparing different training paths. In some environments, particularly those that emphasize extended clinical immersion, therapists accumulate thousands of hours of direct patient contact and supervision, allowing for repeated correction and gradual refinement of their perception. In other training paths, therapists may enter the field with significantly fewer hours of experience and less structured supervision, which makes the transition to independent practice more difficult. The result is that many therapists enter full-time work with strong foundational skills but without a fully developed ability to organize the work efficiently, meaning they are capable, but required to operate at a level that their training has not yet fully supported, which leads to increased effort, increased cognitive load, and a higher risk of burnout.

Understanding this reframes how burnout is interpreted, because it is not primarily a reflection of personal limitation or lack of resilience, but often a reflection of a mismatch between the demands of the work and the level of training that has been provided. When therapists develop the ability to recognize patterns, organize sessions, and maintain clarity under pressure, the experience of the work changes, not because the work itself is easier, but because it is being approached in a way that aligns with how change actually occurs. The difference is not in how much therapists care or how hard they are willing to work, but in how they have been trained to think.

CHAPTER 14 — SUMMARY

- Burnout often reflects a gap between training and the demands of real clinical work
- The core missing skill is pattern recognition under pressure, not knowledge or effort
- Many therapists are trained to understand situations but not to organize them across contexts
- Broad labels like "trauma" or "control" can mask the absence of precise theme identification
- Limited supervision and lack of direct observation slow the development of this skill
- Sustainable practice depends on how therapists are trained to think, not how hard they work

CHAPTER 15

What Happens When You Get This Right

By the time therapists reach this point in their development, something begins to shift in a way that is difficult to fully appreciate until it is experienced. The work itself has not changed in any fundamental way. Patients still bring complex problems, emotionally charged situations, and patterns that are difficult to navigate, and the demands of the profession remain the same. What changes is how the therapist experiences the work.

The sense of being overwhelmed begins to decrease, not because there is less to do, but because the work is more clearly organized. The therapist is no longer pulled in multiple directions by the details of each situation, and instead begins to develop a clearer sense of what matters and what does not. Decisions that once required significant effort begin to feel more straightforward, because they are guided by structure rather than generated in the moment. This change becomes most noticeable in the therapist's thinking, where sessions that once felt mentally heavy begin to feel more focused and more contained.

As this shift continues, the therapist's cognitive load decreases. The therapist is able to listen without becoming overwhelmed by the amount of information being presented and is no longer required to analyze every detail in order to move the session forward. Recognizing patterns allows the work to be organized more efficiently, which reduces the mental effort required to sustain it. The same number of sessions that once felt exhausting begin to feel manageable, not because the work has become easier, but because it is being approached in a way that is more aligned with how change actually occurs.

At the same time, the therapist's emotional experience of the work begins to change. The therapist remains present with the patient's pain but is no longer attempting to control it. There is a shift away from absorbing the emotional weight of each session and toward helping the patient understand and move through it. This creates a form of engagement that is both deeper and more sustainable, because the therapist is no longer carrying what does not belong to them.

The therapist I was supervising experienced this change in a gradual but noticeable way. Sessions that had previously felt disjointed began to feel more connected, not because fewer issues were being discussed, but because those issues were understood as expressions of the same underlying pattern. The urgency to resolve each situation decreased, and the pressure to produce immediate outcomes began to lessen. Instead of feeling responsible for what happened in each session, the therapist began to focus on guiding the process, which allowed the work to feel more stable and more predictable.

This shift also changes how the patient experiences the work. As the therapist maintains clarity and structure, the patient is required to take on a more active role in the process. The patient is no longer relying on the therapist to generate solutions or carry the work forward, but begins to recognize patterns, understand their role within those patterns, and apply new behaviors outside of the session. This leads to more consistent progress, because the work is no longer confined to individual situations but extends across the patient's daily functioning.

Over time, this creates a noticeable change in outcomes. The work becomes less about managing individual problems and more about changing the patterns that produce them. As those patterns begin to shift, the frequency and intensity of the problems decrease. The patient is no longer starting over each week with a new situation, but building on a growing understanding of how to respond differently. The improvement is not dependent on the therapist generating new solutions, but on the patient developing the ability to apply the same understanding across multiple contexts.

Another change becomes apparent in how the therapist relates to the work outside of the session. Sessions no longer follow the therapist in the same way after they end. There is less mental replay, less second-guessing, and less pressure to determine what should have been done differently. The work feels more contained, because it is structured in a way that allows it to be completed within the session. This containment reduces the accumulation of cognitive and emotional strain across the day, allowing the therapist to maintain greater consistency in both attention and energy.

This is what makes the work sustainable over time. It is not that the work becomes easier or less meaningful, but that it becomes more organized. The therapist is no longer compensating for a lack of structure by increasing effort, but is working within a structure that supports clarity, distributes responsibility appropriately, and allows the work to progress without unnecessary strain.

It is also important to recognize what does not change. The work does not become simple. Patients do not stop bringing difficult situations into session, and there are still moments of uncertainty, complexity, and challenge. The therapist still needs to think carefully, respond thoughtfully, and adapt to what is happening in real time. What changes is not the presence of difficulty, but the way that difficulty is managed. When the structure is correct, difficulty becomes something that can be organized and addressed without overwhelming the therapist.

Understanding this shifts how burnout is viewed. Burnout is not an inevitable part of doing meaningful work, nor is it a sign that the therapist is working at a high level. It is an indication that the structure of the work is not aligned with how change actually occurs. When that structure is corrected, the experience of the work changes with it. The therapist becomes more efficient, more focused, and more consistent, while the patient becomes more active and more capable of sustaining progress over time.

In this way, the same work that once felt overwhelming begins to feel manageable, not because less is being done, but because it is being done correctly. The therapist is no longer carrying what does not belong to them, and the patient is no longer dependent on the therapist to move the process forward. The system becomes balanced, and as that balance is maintained, the conditions that produce burnout begin to resolve.

CHAPTER 15 — SUMMARY

- The work becomes more organized, not easier, when the system is correct
- Cognitive load decreases as patterns replace fragmented details
- Emotional burden decreases when therapists stop carrying responsibility for outcomes
- Patients take a more active role and show more consistent progress
- Sessions feel contained, reducing mental carryover and fatigue
- Sustainability emerges from structure, not reduced effort

Final Note

If you were looking for a book that would tell you the solution to burnout is simply to work less, set more boundaries, or reduce your emotional investment in your patients, you may have already noticed that this is not that book. This is not because those ideas are entirely wrong, as there are situations where reducing workload or creating space can provide temporary relief, but because they do not address the underlying structure that produces burnout. Without correcting that structure, the same patterns will continue to return, regardless of how much the workload changes.

This book was written from a different assumption, which is that therapy can be both effective and sustainable, and that burnout is not an unavoidable consequence of doing meaningful work, but a predictable outcome of working in a way that does not align with how change actually occurs. That assumption shifts the focus away from how much work is being done and toward how the work is being approached, which requires a different kind of attention from the therapist.

That shift is not always comfortable. It involves examining how you work, not just how hard you work, and it may challenge ideas that have felt intuitive or appropriate in the moment. It also requires recognizing that some approaches that feel compassionate or helpful in the short term may not produce consistent results over time, which is not a criticism of the therapist, but a reflection of how the work is commonly structured and taught. For some readers, this perspective will align naturally with their experience, while for others it may take time to integrate, particularly if it differs from how they have been trained or how they have understood their work up to this point.

The ideas in this book are not meant to stand alone. They are meant to be applied, observed, and refined through experience. As you continue working, you may begin to recognize the patterns described here more quickly, notice when the work becomes disorganized, and identify when responsibility begins to shift in ways that increase effort without improving outcomes. More importantly, you will begin to recognize how to correct those shifts as they occur.

That process is not immediate, and it does not eliminate the complexity of the work. Patients will continue to bring difficult situations into session, and there will still be moments of uncertainty and challenge, but when the structure of the work is clear, the therapist is able to engage with that complexity without becoming overwhelmed by it.

Burnout is not reduced by working less. It is reduced by working correctly. When the structure of the work is aligned with how change actually occurs, the therapist no longer carries what does not belong to them, the patient becomes responsible for their role in the process, and the work becomes both more effective and more sustainable over time. This is not a different kind of therapy, but a more precise way of doing the same work, organized in a way that allows both the therapist and the patient to function at a higher level.

References

Van Hoy, A., & Rzeszutek, M. (2022). Burnout and psychological wellbeing among psychotherapists: A systematic review. *Frontiers in Psychology, 13*, 928191. https://doi.org/10.3389/fpsyg.2022.928191

Dewa, C. S., Loong, D., Bonato, S., Thanh, N. X., & Jacobs, P. (2017). How does burnout affect mental health professionals? A systematic review. *Clinical Practice and Epidemiology in Mental Health, 13*, 1–16.

Morse, G., Salyers, M. P., Rollins, A. L., Monroe-DeVita, M., & Pfahler, C. (2012). Burnout in mental health services: A review of the problem and its remediation. *Administration and Policy in Mental Health and Mental Health Services Research, 39*(5), 341–352.

Sánchez-Moreno, E., De La Fuente, R., Gallardo-Peralta, L. P., Barrón-López de Roda, A., & Panadero, S. (2015). Burnout, social support, and self-esteem in social workers and mental health professionals. *Journal of Social Service Research, 41*(3), 365–377.

Simionato, G. K., & Simpson, S. (2018). Personal risk factors associated with burnout among psychotherapists: A systematic review. *Journal of Clinical Psychology, 74*(7), 1085–1101.

Winstanley, S., & White, E. (2011). The relationship between burnout, depression, and social support among school mental health workers. *School Psychology Quarterly, 26*(2), 125–136.

Delgadillo, J., Saxon, D., & Barkham, M. (2018). Associations between therapists' occupational burnout and their patients' depression and anxiety treatment outcomes. *Depression and Anxiety, 35*(9), 844–850. https://doi.org/10.1002/da.22766

Sayer, N. A., Kaplan, A., Nelson, D. B., Wiltsey Stirman, S., & Rosen, C. S. (2024). Clinician burnout and effectiveness of guideline-recommended psychotherapies. *JAMA Network Open, 7*(4), e246858. https://doi.org/10.1001/jamanetworkopen.2024.6858

Bes, I., Shoman, Y., Al-Gobari, M., Rousson, V., & Guseva Canu, I. (2023). Organizational interventions and occupational burnout: A meta-analysis with focus on exhaustion. *International Archives of Occupational and*

Environmental Health, 96(9), 1211–1223. https://doi.org/10.1007/s00420-023-02009-z

Index